C000008525

Change Your Mind
Change Your Life

Mark L. Morris

Introduction

Do you dream of being the CEO of a Fortune 500 company? Have you wanted to buy that new home you've dreamed of for so many years? Exactly what is your idea of success?

Success is having achieved that which you determine you will do!

YOU determine what success is for you. It's not based on any judgment other than your own. It's not dependent upon materialistic measurements. And, for some, success is the journey, itself.

Success may be something material, such as money or a new home. It could be something egotistical, as the power and notoriety that comes with the position of CEO. It could be emotional, as finding love and commitment. Success may even be unselfish and altruistic, as seeing children in third world countries healthy and safe. Success has no particular name or identity. There is no one method to describe what success is, other than the definition above. It means something different to each individual.

All successful people, however, have one thing in common — determination! To be a success, you must first determine to be so. Though not always a conscious decision, the seed that leads to action is *to first determine.*

Diane's story is a great example of having a desire in the conscious mind, and the subconscious processing it as a determination. Diane's love of writing began in middle school, because her friends were writing short romance stories about their favorite music idols. Diane thought she would give it a try. Her stories became so popular that she began writing them in segments. Her classmates couldn't wait to get the next installment. From that point, she wrote different types of things — poetry, philosophy, and sometimes only her thoughts. She won a few writing competitions in school, but most of her writings were for herself. It was only a hobby. Something she did to pass time, or a way to put her thoughts on paper. When she entered college, she didn't give writing a second thought. She graduated with a dual degree in psychology and business management. Diane worked in business for several years; then, "fell" into the writing profession.

She thought it just happened; but in truth, each position she held had some writing responsibilities — first, business reports and editing manuals, then putting together and writing a monthly newsletter for the firm. At the job she "fell" into, she started as a secretary, after having moved to another state. Being used to a heavier workload, they finally gave her a small job to do for their technical writer, who was writing an employee handbook for the firm. Between her regular duties, Diane, who had written a similar handbook at her previous job, filled in the gaps, extended the contents so the handbook was complete, and gave a draft to the technical writer for review. Her assignment was only to lay out what he'd written. To make a long story short, they offered her a job as a proposal writer, and then a position as their engineering documentation coordinator, where she wrote customized engineering manuals. Though it seemed to Diane that she "fell" into the job of professional writing, she had "determined" it years before while writing those short stories in middle school. She has now been writing professionally for over 20 years, including books and novels. When I once asked her why she didn't just go to school for English or Journalism, she said she never thought about it. Her love was psychology. She considered herself to be a halfway decent writer and always believed she would write on some level. She didn't discount writing professionally; it just never crossed her mind.

So, what was Diane's problem? Though on a subconscious level, she had "determined" to be a writer. Why did it take so long? Because there was no clear goal in which ...

to believe!

Being successful is a two-part process — determination and belief! Both of which begin in the mind. Diane was fortunate that her determination to write became a career. She began to believe, because the determination was creating opportunities — her bosses praised her writing and gave her more, college professors praised her abilities, and once a man wept after having read one of her poems. That's when she began to believe in her ability to write. She began to believe she had talent — if she hadn't, she would not be a writer today. It was enough to thrust her forward to enter the profession her heart desired. She might have achieved her success much sooner had she been consciously working toward it.

It's important to be consciously on your path to success, and equally important to prepare your mind, spirit and body for the success you seek. It's not enough to be an anonymous member of society, who lets others decide your fate. To allow life to "pull you along" creates conflicts, resentments and lost opportunities. Without a clear notion of where you want to be means that you:

- **End up in situations not to your liking**. Why? Because if you don't have a clear idea of what you want in life, you get whatever is left over, causing conflicts by not having what you believe you desire but never determined, being in one bad relationship after another, being in one bad job after another, and so on.

- **Resent your life and many of the people in it**. This isn't what you imagined for yourself! In truth, if you had taken the time to truly imagine something for yourself and went beyond dreaming and wanting it to determining and believing, you would be there now and would not be reading this book.

- **Pass up many opportunities** that could help you get to where you're going faster. You don't take risks — you play it safe. Why? You don't recognize the opportunities as such, when they present themselves.

The chapters that follow show you the steps to take to change your life NOW! We teach you how to be consciously on your path. It's never too late to start.

The principles herein are used for any type of success you seek, regardless of what it is.

So, get ready to open yourself to new opportunities and to succeed in any way you desire — you can be anything at any time, anywhere. You only need to open your mind to the possibilities, then ... **Change Your Mind — Change Your Life!**

> "If you think you can or
> You think you can't,
> You are always right!"
>
> Henry Ford

Open Your Mind to the Possibilities

Determination and belief are the starting points for success. They open you to new opportunities to do and be anything you desire, and you only need a subconscious thought to plant the seed. How do we do this?

The first and most important element of success is to ...

open your mind.

A closed mind seals off creative solutions and eliminates any possibility for new opportunities. A closed mind keeps you where you are in life, where you always have been, and will continue to be. A closed mind creates:

- Constant struggle to achieve or get ahead,

- Constant conflicts and obstacles, the ever-present resentments that rear their ugly heads for each new situation you encounter,

- Remorse of not doing or having what you truly dream, and

- The envy you feel each time you meet, read or hear about someone more successful than you, knowing you should be in that person's shoes.

None of these feelings are conducive to success. Envision wild horses pent up in a corral. They yearn to be free. As long as the fences are up and the gate is locked, the wild horses that desire freedom more than life, itself, will never be free. What does this do to them? They become angry and willing to trample the person who caged them, just to get free. They blame and resent their keeper for their situation. Each time they see other horses roaming free in the distance, all their anger, resentment and hatred surfaces; and they envy the freedom of the other horses. Now, see these wild horses as you and your dream for success, corralled and caged by your closed mind. Can you see how, as the horses, you become angry, resentful, hating, and envious? Can you see how a closed mind and the emotions it provokes affect your reactions to situations? Wild horses will kill their keeper for freedom and react viciously at seeing other horses that are free. What reactions do you have to situations, where you feel anger, resentment or blame?

All the horses need to gain their freedom is to unlock and open the gate. All you need do to be on your path to achieving success is to **open your mind**.

When you truly open your mind, the anger, resentments, hatred and envy are gone; however, it takes some work on your part. Let's look at how the mind works.

A thought, just like an action, is energy in motion. Emotional thoughts carry even more energy. When you create a thought, especially one you feel emotional about (such as your dream of success), you have created energy that goes out to the universe[1] and allows you to explore, create and grow the thought. The process takes care of itself.

We all have thoughts, but we don't all achieve our dreams. That's because **thoughts may be**

---

[1] We use the term "universe" in this book to include all readers. The term could just as easily be God, Allah, Yahweh, or any other source you believe controls this universe in which we live.

negative or positive in nature. Even thoughts you believe are positive may, in truth, be negative to achievement. For example, your dream is to own a new home. The thought you constantly hold is, "I want to buy a new home." This sounds like a positive thought, but it's actually keeping you from getting your new home. Why? The phrase "I want" keeps you *wanting* to buy a new home, rather than actually buying it. So, you continue to want to buy it — never achieving your goal.

Focus is another problem in how thoughts are formulated in our thoughts. You constantly think about that new home you "want" to buy. You look at different homes and floor plans, comb the "for sale" home classifieds, pick out the color you'll paint the outside, look at landscaping ideas, and so on. You would believe that this is a positive focus, because it keeps the goal constantly in your mind and you actions are that of someone who is buying a new home. The problem, however, is that the focus is on "getting" versus "doing". Rather than moving toward your goal, you are dreaming about it.

(We'll cover both of these negative thought patterns, as well as other elements covered in this chapter, and how to make them positive in the chapter entitled, "Rewriting Your Reality". Here, we want to emphasize the power of your mind, and how thoughts create your reality.)

With an open mind, you plant the seed, distance yourself from it, and let the universe do the rest. You must, however, be open to all possibilities without exception. **That means only positive thinking, no attachments, and no labeling.**

An open and positive mind allows the universe to act upon your inner thought energy and create that which you seek. It's like watching a little miracle take place. It can astound you, when you realize it's happening.

> *Years ago, after a divorce from a financially irresponsible spouse, Beth wrote down goals for her children and herself — to have enough food on the table, a good roof over their heads, and a decent car to drive in ten years. Many years later, she was preparing to close on a townhouse and had just picked up a new car. Then, it hit her — she remembered those long-ago goals that she hadn't even thought of since. She counted the years and was amazed.*

The closing on her house would be exactly two months shy of ten years from the divorce date. Beth realized then that she should have written in five years instead of ten!

As you can see, distancing yourself from the goals and just working toward them brings success. Beth determined; then, she believed, because she could do no less for her children. She just kept working to do better. The process took care of itself. Yet, Beth never saw it coming, until it already had arrived. However, Beth probably missed a lot of opportunities along the way and went through a lot more struggle, because she wasn't consciously moving toward her goals.

Let's look at some elements of thinking that hold us back from consciously moving toward success.

Energy Expands

Your thoughts become energy. If your thoughts are negative, the energy is negative; if positive, then the energy is positive. When emotions become involved with the thoughts, the energy is even stronger. The energy, however, doesn't remain dormant — it expands. It expands each time you think your thought. Remember our example, "I want to buy a new home." The more you think this thought, the energy expands and builds, and the stronger the thought becomes. Dreaming of your "want" builds the energy more.

As energy builds and gains strength, it begins to attract like energy. Like a magnet, the energy attracts other like matter to it. Since the energy is inside you, it attracts the like matter to you. If your thoughts lean toward the negative, then you are attracting negative matter — dead end jobs, horrible bosses, bad relationships, never achieving that which you most want, constant struggle, conflicts, built up anger, and so on. Whereas, if your thoughts are positive, you attract positive outcomes and situations.

As you can see, negative thoughts and energy weaken you and your ability to achieve. Positive thoughts and energy empower you. Whatever you think, you attract back to you in greater degrees. Literally, your thoughts do create your reality. Evidence is all around you. Are your thoughts negative or positive? Do negative or positive situations, events and people surround you?

Beyond Thoughts. If your thoughts and the energy attached to them are negative, what type of speech and actions will you put forth? Negative! What is inside you (thoughts) is how you respond to life. If your thoughts are negative, then your speech and actions are negative, too. Likewise, if your thoughts are positive, then so is your speech and actions, which also add to the building and attracting of like energy.

> *For example, if you keep "wanting" to buy a new home, you become frustrated, angry and begin to blame others for not achieving your goal — not paid enough at work, lenders won't give you a break, and so on. These emotions spill out into your speech and actions, especially your reactions. A lender turns you down, and you become angry. He might have planned to tell you what you needed to do to become eligible or suggest a particular lender who might be able to help, but you blew up and took your frustration out on him.*

This is called a missed opportunity ... all because the negative built internally, spilled out at the wrong time, and at the wrong person. Your thoughts not only define your reality, but they define who you are and how you act, as well.

Enculturation Programming

Another element of thinking and having an open mind is our programming through enculturation. Enculturation is our environment from the time of our birth to this moment. It includes our culture, friends, the people we have met along the way, family (especially, our parents), authority encounters (teachers, police officers, etc.), education — virtually every person, place or thing we have encountered within our lifetime!

That's a lot of influence, and this influence has a way of programming our minds to be something other than who we truly are. It causes prejudices, dislikes, and believing certain things are "right" while others are "wrong". It leaves many choices unexplored, many opportunities missed, and many pathways labeled as "wrong".

Enculturation programming, especially at an early age by your parents and family, enable you to fit within your culture, your community, and the type of life they expect you will have. It's done with the best of intentions. Some is done outwardly. Some is subconscious. Most is done, because their parents did it to them. We accept it in our youth, rebel against it in our teens, and usually do it to our own children because it helped us turn out okay.

Some of this programming is necessary to keep us safe, healthy and sane. However, a lot of it clogs our thinking and suppresses creativity. It's this part that causes a closed mind, holding you back and keeping you attached to the past. Once you can let go of this programming, doors of possibility and success open to you.

A lot of this mental programming is easy to recognize. Each has a recorded tape that runs in your mind. Do you ever catch yourself sounding just like your mother or father? Say a phrase your grandmother always said? Do something, because someone else always did it that way? Feel a particular way about someone or something, because that's the correct way to feel? Become repulsed by something, because you've always felt that way? These are all programming tapes. You need to begin recognizing them and eliminating them from your mind.

Programming causes attachments to the past —
essentially, attachment to the programming that
was done in the past. These attachments cause
negative thoughts, limiting self-speech, limiting
actions and responses, and the need to "be right".
None of these traits are conducive to being open
or to achieve your goals.

Self-Speech. This is what we mentally say to
ourselves and to others about ourselves. It limits
us by our own self-labels.

> *"I'm not good enough to do that job."*
> *"I'm not attractive enough to get that girl
> to date me."*
> *"I'm too shy."*
> *"I always fail at that."*
> *"My father was right. I'll never amount to
> much."*
> *"My pastor says we're not deserving of
> good things. God will provide
> what He will for me."*

These are only a fraction of the negative things
we say to ourselves. You could probably list many
pages of your own limiting self-speech. Most
comes from our programming, as the examples
above. From there, we create our own negative

labels about ourselves. In this wonderful world in which we live, it's amazing how very few people truly like themselves. Their self-speech defines them, just as surely as it defines their reality. It's called a ...

self-fulfilling prophecy — you say you are, and so you become!

Self-fulfilling prophecies, usually from your early programming, causes the doubt and fear whenever you wish to take a leap of faith and risk something. They pull you back to your comfort zone and keep you in your corral. They keep your expectations for yourself, others and events low, including limiting your capabilities, talent, potential and opportunities. They keep you from listening to crazy schemes that just could be your path to success. *Your parents would never have considered such schemes, and you're not about to either!*

Need to Be Right. This is a symptom of attachments and enculturation programming, generally from a very influential person, such as a parent. Whether you believe it or not, you have to be right! The programming is so strong that it's a conditioned reflex. You'll argue your point until you're blue in the face. Ever have a time when you wondered why you argued about the topic at all — it wasn't even important to you afterward, or you could actually see the other person's point? This is a result of programming; and unfortunately, doesn't make you many new friends (unless, they are forced to be around you).

To have an open mind and achieve your goals, you must let go of this need to be right, the limiting self-speech, the programming, and the negative thoughts. You may determine to achieve a goal, but all of this negativeness will keep you from believing it.

Exercises

You cannot develop an open mind without a bit of mental work. We provide exercises at the end of each chapter to help you. The results of the exercises you do here are used in later exercises. Don't worry about your answers — no one else need see them. Be as honest as you can be. It will assist you greatly to take a spiral notepad and use as a journal for this work. You may find it helpful in later months to have your notes to review from time to time.

Exercise #1 — Examine Your Thoughts

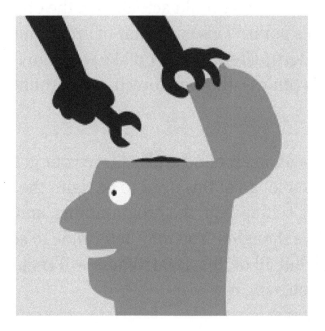

Look at your current situation and the success you seek.

- **Write down in your journal your success goal** (if you have several, choose only one for the exercise and use it for all the exercises within this book).

- Make several copies of the table on page 16.

- For the next seven days (do not skip any days), **jot down all negative thoughts, speech and actions** you have in the first column of your table, whether you believe they may affect your goal or not. Use as many pages of tables as needed. At first, you won't always catch yourself. As the week passes, you'll begin catching your negative thoughts, speech and actions more often.

Negative	Programming	Self-Speech	Need to Be Right
	What: Who: Truth:		
	What: Who: Truth:		

Exercise #2 — The Influence of Programming

Using the table from Exercise #1, do the following:

- For each negative listed in column one, determine if it came from programming, from whom, and how you may have caused the situation.

- Then, determine what **self-speech** you contribute to keeping this programming alive within your life and why you **need to be right** about it. Begin the "need to be right" statement with, "If I'm not right, then ..." The example continues on the next page.

See an example of a completed table on the next page.

Once you have completed all the exercises in the book, you may wish to continue Exercises #1 and #2, until you begin to see the negative thoughts, speech and actions substantially decrease. Keep them in your journal.

Negative	Programming	Self-Speech	Need to Be Right
I like this guy, but he won't notice me.	**What:** Guys don't like me, because they never asked me out. **Who:** My mother always told others how shy I was, and I always reacted with shyness. **Truth:** Maybe I wasn't asked out, because they never had a chance to know Me?	I'm too shy to meet guys.	**If I'm not right, then** they have a chance to get to know me, and they may not like me because I'm ugly or something equally depressing.

I could do my boss' job better than him! Who does he think he is?	**What:** I was always taught that people who earned their living worked hard. This guy doesn't do much of anything. **Who:** My father, who worked in a steel mill all his life. **Truth:** My father was stuck in his job, because he didn't have the resources or drive to rise above it. I don't truly know everything my boss does.	I have to work hard to get ahead, even if that means working extra hours each week — whether it's needed or not.	**If I'm not right, then** I have to admit that I feel under-appreciated in this job. Then, I'd have to face the prospect of hunting for a new job, which I detest.

Who Are You?

To develop an open mind, it's essential to take an honest look at who you truly are. It's a difficult question to answer. You may believe you know, but seldom do you truly know without outside input. In 1955, Joseph Luft and Harry Ingham developed the Johari Window, named for both their first names of Joseph and Harry. The Johari Window helps you to better understand your personality.

The Window is made up of four panes, representing the four areas of personality.

1. Only You Know	2. You Show to Others
That part of yourself that only you know	That part of yourself that you know and share with others
3. Only Others Know	**4. No One Knows**
That part of yourself that others see, but that you are unaware of its existence	That part of yourself that no one knows — not yourself or others

Quadrant #1 — Only You Know. This is the area of yourself that you do not wish to disclose to anyone else. It's the very private and vulnerable part of your personality that holds your fears and doubts. It holds any embarrassing or hurtful event that you did or has happened to you. You choose very carefully whom you allow to know this part of you, if anyone at all.

Quadrant #2 — You Show to Others. This is the area of your personality that you share with others in varying degrees, depending upon your trust level with each individual. You feel safe and confident with this part of your personality and the information contained in this quadrant. People are welcome here.

Quadrant #3 — Only Others Know. Though you may not be aware, there is a part of your personality, information about you, which other people know, but you do not. This quadrant holds that part of you. Such knowledge may be bad habits you do without knowing, such as the habit of biting your lip when you're unsure of something. Maybe, something like the follow example.

Dan didn't realize until he was video taped that, when he speaks, hr looks like he's waving down a freight train. He knew he used his hands for emphasis, but Dan never suspected that he used his hands to such an extent.

Knowledge in this quadrant also may be your potential. Sometimes, others see in us, what we don't see in ourselves. These are just a few examples. So many things may reside in this quadrant for you.

Quadrant #4 — No One Knows. This area holds any knowledge and potential that you or anyone else has yet to discover. Science has proven that we use only a small portion of our brain's capacity. Some things from this quadrant, you will discover between now and when you leave this world. The majority of it, you will never know. The fourth quadrant also is the area where dreams are made real, where new theories are born, where new science is first thought and then discovered, and where creativity is given birth. New thought develops here. New ideas that change the world develop here. It's the unknown part of you ... the creative part of you.

How Does This Apply to You? We've already shown why it's important to know more about you. In the last chapter, we began working in Quadrant #1 of the Johari Window in Exercises #1 and #2. To truly answer the question, "Who are you?, you need to know as much about all four quadrants as possible. To be truly open, you need an unflinching self-assessment in order to take full responsibility for who you are and where you are on your path of life.

Exercises

Exercise #3 — Who Are You, Quadrant #1

- Make eight copies of the table on the next page. Put seven copies aside.

- On the remaining copy, complete the table, using ten words or phrases (both negative and positive) to describe each area of yourself and your personality.

Exercise #4 — Who Are You, Quadrant #2, Part 1

- Using another copy of the table, complete it again as you believe others see you.

- You should now have two tables completed with six blank tables remaining. Store the completed copies of the tables for Exercises #3 and #4 in your journal for now.

Insert 10 words/phrases that describe:

Physical Appearance	Temperament (mood)	Personality	Behaviors (good/bad)	Philosophy of Life	Total Overall Person

Exercise #5 — Who Are You, Quadrant #2, Part 2

- Now, choose five individuals that you would like to know how they feel about you, and one truly close friend/relative that you trust. Of the five individuals, some should be coworkers, a boss, close friends and/or relatives. Mix it up a bit. You want a range of people with whom you associate.

- Meet with the close, trusted friend/relative, and tell him/her what you are doing. "I'm participating in a workshop on self-growth" is a good example, with details of what the other five people will be asked to do. Ask if he/she would be willing to have envelopes mailed to them to collate into a similar table, destroy the five tables received in the mail, and then giving the collated table to you. Give a copy of the table to your trusted friend/relative to use for collating the information received.

- Fold the five remaining copies of the table and insert into generic, **stamped** envelopes addressed to your close friend/ relative (there should be no way to differentiate between the envelopes or copies of the tables). Put the close friend/ relative's address as the return address, too.

- Meet with each of the five chosen individuals, again explaining what you are doing. Ask each of them if they would complete the table about you. Ensure they know that the envelope is going to a friend/ relative to collate, and they are not to put their names on either the paper or the envelope. Ask them to complete the table and mail it within five days. Be sure to thank them for their time and assistance.

  (If anyone declines, choose someone else, who is in a similar position as that person — whether friend or someone with whom you work.)

- After you receive the collated table from your trusted friend/relative, block off some personal and private time to review the results. Don't get angry over any comments. Remember, these are honest thoughts on how others view you and important for you to know. Also, don't

worry about who said what — that isn't
important here.

- Were there any surprises? Make notes in
  your journal of your thoughts or feelings.

- Now, compare the collated responses to the
  two tables you previously completed. Were
  their responses closest to the table you
  completed in Exercises #3 and #4? Did
  they know you better than you thought they
  did? Or, did they give the type of responses
  you thought they would?

- Make notes in your journal of all the traits
  in the collated table that matches the traits
  from Exercises #3 and #4. These validate
  that these are definitely part of who you
  are. The collated responses answer
  Quadrant #2 of the Johari Window, "You
  Show to Others".

- Now, everything that remains in the
  collated table should be things you didn't
  know about yourself — whether you agree
  with the statements or not. Write these in
  your journal, noting that these are
  Quadrant #3 of the Johari Window.

Exercise #6 — Who Are You?

- In this last exercise, review the three tables and the information you have gained within them.

- Now, write down on paper **who you are**. Use all the words and phrases within each of the three tables, including any with which you disagree. Use as many pages as you like. You don't have to complete the description in one sitting. You can do this over a couple of days, returning to the writing periodically.

You want a complete and thorough description of YOU.

- When finished, put the description in your journal. Note in journal what you have learned from the exercises in this chapter. How did they help you?

Rewrite Your Reality

In the last chapter, we looked at the Johari Window and three of its quadrants. Now, we will work in Quadrant #4. This is the part of your personality that no one knows. It's that part of you that holds the infinite possibilities for success. We may not know what's in this area, but we do know that it's the area that creates with the universe, processes, and achieves success.

To rewrite your reality, you must reinvent yourself. To do this, you need to change your thinking, your speech, and your actions/ reactions. **You cannot change the current life your mind created, with the same mind that created it.** You must change the way you think. Change your mind — change your reality.

We've already touched on the mental elements that you need to address — enculturation programming, your need to be right, negativity and self-speech. Now, we'll show you how to change your mind by changing these obstacles to success.

Programming

You know what programming is and why it's detrimental to achieving your dream. In Exercise #2, you should have determined what some of your programming is. We all have a lot of programming by the time we're grown. It's a continual process to rid ourselves of this, as well as new programming that is thrust upon us as adults. Just remember, though you may be doing everything correctly in your life, you didn't write that rulebook — someone else did. Now, it's time to write your own.

You first want to give up your history. That doesn't mean to deny who you are within your family or culture. It means to let go of the programming and the negative cyclical events that have further programmed you.

For example, you keep ending up in dead end jobs with abusive bosses.
By now, you believe that you'll never get out of the rut.
You'll never get a job you love with a great boss.

This is a negative cyclical event that further programs you in a negative manner; because if you believe you'll never find the perfect job, then you won't. Remember, the *Introduction* quote from Henry Ford — *If you think you can or if you think you can't, you are always right.*

The past does not drive you forward, unless you allow it. Just because things have progressed a specific way up until now, doesn't mean it must continue to do so. Allowing a negative cyclical event to control your future makes you a victim.

By allowing your programming to continue, you empower your past instead of your present. You hold onto old habits, beliefs, and self-defeating behaviors.

Cherish the good you remember from your past — the events, feelings and people. Confront and accept the bad, because nothing happens in our lives by accident. Regardless of how bad things may have been in your past, you wouldn't be the person you are now without this past and the events it holds. You had to go through all that you did to be YOU.

You are not what you've done, what you've been, how others have taught you, or what has been done to you. Your past and all its hurts are no longer in this reality, unless you allow them to be here to continue to cause hurts, conflicts, and negative cyclical events. You cannot change your past, but you can change your response to it.

Changing Programming. Each time you recognize programming in your thinking, write it down on paper, determine from whom the programming came, mentally thank the individual (this removes any negative feelings you may have), write a new response for your future.

> *Continuing with our examples in Exercise #2:*

> **Programming:** *Others and I were always told I was shy.*
> **Who:** *My mother*
> **New Programming:** *I am not a shy person. I love people and work to ensure they are comfortable, just in case they are shy.*

Programming: I was always taught that people who earned their living worked hard. This guy doesn't do much of anything.
Who: My father
New Programming: Working "smarter" (not harder) makes me a success.

Now, use the response as affirmations, and tape them on something (like the bathroom mirror) that you'll see each morning and evening. Then, make a point to read all of your affirmations, when you first awake and just before going to sleep. Do not remove an affirmation, until it is a belief that you not only believe in your mind but you reflect in your speech and reaction/actions, as well.

This is giving up your past and eliminating your programming.

Time, the Immobilizer

Another obstacle to an open mind and achieving success is an off-shoot of programming. That obstacle is Time!

Time can be our biggest enemy. We try to reclaim the past. We avoid the challenges and pressures of today. And we worry about what the future may bring.

We have all met someone who lives in the past. Terry was an old friend from high school. It's been over 20 years, and the guy still cannot let go of his glory days as captain of the football team and all the adoration that was showered upon him. He was picked up by a pro football team but was in a car accident right before training started. Terry blew his knee, which effectively ended his career as a football star. He does everything possible to forget the car accident that ended his career, instead reliving his high school days. It's cost Terry his family and any decent career, since nothing is as good as the glory days. He cannot see all that he is missing in life. He's alone and an alcoholic.

47

The truly sad thing is that Terry's a really nice guy, but he can't even see that.

What about a person who lives for the future?

The woman who is still waiting for her true love and refuses to move on with her life.

The guy who moves from one big scheme after the other, dreaming of the day he's rich.

The guy who's still pining for his ex-wife, waiting for the day she returns (it's only been ten years).

The woman who puts most her paycheck into lottery tickets, dreaming of making a killing and letting her bills go.

These people and many more are missing out on the present, just like Terry. They, too, lose opportunities for relationships and career successes. And as focused as they are on the past or a future that hasn't arrived (always wanting), they will never be happy in this life, nor will they succeed at what they desire — your cannot redo the past in the present, and always wanting something in the future keeps pushing it away from you, keeping you "wanting".

All we truly have is now — today! The past is gone, and the future has yet to arrive. Living in either the past or future causes you to lose the now.

Now is when you can make a difference in your life, not the past or future. Now is where you find happiness and inner peace. Now is where you enjoy what the universe has given you — family, friends, and whatever brings you joy. They may not be there tomorrow. NOW is the place to plant seeds for tomorrow's success.

Devote a section of your journal to time. Whenever you notice yourself living in the past or future, make a note of it. Write down the thought. Then, revise it for the present:

Terry reliving his glory days — revision for the present:
My high school sports taught me leadership ability, teamwork, and how to succeed. I will make notes on how these

lessons can help me in my present, my now.

Living in the past? It's in the past. Good or bad, confront and accept it, then deal with the present only. View the past as a milestone for your current success, which is only a milestone toward your ultimate goal.

The woman waiting for her true love — revision for the present:

I know my true love will manifest himself in my life, when I'm ready for a loving relationship and commitment. In the meantime, I will live my life, developing friendships, dating without immediately evaluating the man as a possible husband, and buying that home I've wanted. When my true love is here, I will offer him a whole woman with a full life.

Do you perceive problems will happen or are you "wanting" something? Distance yourself from such thinking. Instead, focus on something positive in the here and now.

Continually be aware of your state of thinking, which affects your speech and actions. Don't allow the past or "wants" of the future to immobilize you in your present.

Need to Be Right

In Exercise #2, you noted the times when you felt you had to be right. Be alert to these times. Begin to catch yourself doing this, while it's happening. Then,

- Tell yourself that nothing in the universe is personal. It's only energy moving back and forth. So, don't take life, the people or events so seriously.

- When someone attacks you personally, they wish to anger you. They are upset over something (which may have nothing to do with you) and have built up a lot of negative energy inside. They wish to feel better; and, in order to do so, they must release the negative energy. You are their target. As long as you don't react negatively and keep a positive posture, then the other person retains the negative energy.

Here are some ideas to help you change the conditioned reflex of needing to be right:

- Change how you view yourself.

  - Compare Exercises #3 and #6. What is difference between the two? What did others tell you about yourself that you didn't know?

  - Relish the nice things you learned about yourself. Be sure to feel good (not egotistical) about yourself, whenever you project such traits.

- Of the traits that were less than favorable, don't ignore them or not agree. Review the one success goal you chose earlier. Could these unfavorable traits inhibit your path to success? Be honest. You need not tell anyone about them, but you can turn them into opportunities for growth. Write them down on paper in one column. In a second column, write what you can do to change them to positives. Then, begin working on them (just don't try to do everything at once, you'll become overwhelmed).

- Now, compare Exercises #4 and #5. Were you projecting to others the image you thought or wanted to project?

    Sara is a very outgoing and direct person and believed she appears as aggressive and controlling when people first meet her. She thought her coworkers saw her this way. When she did this exercise, she was pleasantly surprised to find that all five people knew she was an outgoing but non-controlling person, who spoke very directly. Even two individuals, with whom Sara worked only occasionally, knew this.

We hope your experience was as positive as Sara's. If it wasn't and your "others" see you negatively when you thought you were projecting a positive image, then you need to be unflinching honest with yourself. You've been closing your eyes. In the future, pay closer attention to how people react to you. If you're seeing signs of negative reactions, ask the people about it.

The purpose of this exercise isn't to conform to the expectations of others. You are not your reputation. You are not who others believe you are. However, at this point in "changing your mind to change your life", you need as much information as you can get. The Johari Window gives you a lot of input about where you currently are that wouldn't be available otherwise. It

also lets you evaluate personal traits
that may be hindering your success.

- Be happy and at peace. Too often we
  believe that if some event (i.e. win the
  lottery, meet our true love) happens, we'll
  be happy or at peace. The problem is that
  as soon as you gain what you seek, you
  soon become disappointed, disillusioned
  and dissatisfied again. You probably won't
  even know why. It's because you have
  attached conditions to your happiness and
  peace. You do not bring to you or receive
  from someone or something else happiness
  and peacefulness.

  No one and nothing can make you happy or
  at peace. You either are, or you're not. You
  decide to be happy, and you decide to be at
  peace. Again, it's a determination and
  belief. Once you determine that you are
  happy and at peace, you act in happiness
  and peace. When a negative situation
  presents itself, just remind yourself that
  you are happy and at peace. It allows you a
  moment to mentally step back from the
  situation and find a positive reaction.

- Be open-minded in all situations. Respond to new situations, ideas and knowledge with an open mind. To keep the "need to be right" at bay, say to yourself,

> *"I may never have thought*
> *of this before or in this way.*
> *I want to listen without*
> *comment, even if it's only to*
> *learn more about this*
> *person who is speaking."*

You will find that people become more interesting. You begin to enjoy conversations again. And people begin to engage you in conversation more often.

- When you encounter a person who believes there is only one way to do something and is determined to make you see this and agree, keep the following in mind:

  - Compared to the vast universe, this conversation has very little meaning.

  - Whether you agree or not, if the person truly believes what he or she is saying, then:

- You won't change their mind, regardless of what you say.

- If they believe it, then it is TRUE for THEM, and it doesn't affect you or who you are.

- When you see the conversation isn't going anywhere, look for an opening. Then say, "You're right. I'm glad we discussed this." Or, "Sounds interesting. I'm glad you mentioned it." Then, walk away and don't allow the topic to resurface again.

Negative Energy

In the first chapter, we discussed how negative energy weakens you and positive energy empowers you. In Exercise #1, you kept a list of negative thoughts, speech or actions you experienced for seven days. In this chapter, you have learned how to reprogram your thinking, the importance of time and living in the now versus the past or future, and how to overcome the need to be right. Once you have changed these traits, you still will be dealing with negative energy. That's because it becomes a habit, and the habit must be changed. Let's look at the graphic on the next page.

1 = Conscious part of the brain

A & B = The subconscious
part of the brain — the warehouse of thought

A = Readily Accessible Memory (RAM)

B = Stored information but not accessible
without a "key" to open the door (Cold Storage)

As we allow negative or positive thoughts into
our mind, they are stored in the brain. What we
have most recently thought is in the conscious
section (1).

As we continue to have thoughts, eventually the
older thoughts in section 1 are pushed into the
subconscious, specifically to the front of the
warehouse or RAM section (A). To make room
for these thoughts, the older thoughts already in
RAM are then pushed into Cold Storage (B).

To access RAM thoughts, you need only have the
desire to do so, and the thoughts are
automatically again in the conscious section of

your brain (1) for use. Access is almost immediately. The slight delay is negligible.

To access Cold Storage (B) thoughts, however, is more difficult. It takes a key to open the door. Deja vu[2] is an example of a key. Reminiscing with an old friend will bring up memories (thoughts) you haven't remembered for ages. How many times have you thought or said, "It's on the tip of my tongue," yet you never quite bring a thought to the forefront? This is an example of a key to the Cold Storage area of your brain — sometimes, the key is strong enough to open the door; sometimes, it isn't.

As negative energy builds, your thoughts, speech and actions become more negative more often in direct proportion with the negative energy inside you, as well as the negative energy surrounding you. As your negative thoughts grow, they push the positive thoughts (you used to have) into the RAM portion of the warehouse. Eventually, they're at the back of Cold Storage.

---

[2] The illusion of remembering scenes and events when experienced for the first time; a
feeling that you have seen, heard or felt something before.

What does this do to your thoughts and internal energy? It attracts more of the same. Eventually, any positive thoughts are long forgotten, and you seldom find a key to unlock their door. This is the effect of negative thinking, which is far reaching into your future — unless you stop it right here, right now.

To stop this snowball effect, you must change what's inside you to positive. As you can see from the graphic, the only way to change what's already there (negative) is to replace it with positive thoughts. You must avoid all thoughts that weaken you (negative). To do this,

- Become more aware of your thoughts by continuing to do Exercise #1. The more you pay attention to your thoughts, the more you'll become aware of them. Eventually, you'll be able to stop such thoughts in your mind, before they become speech or actions.

- Each time you catch yourself thinking something negative, stop and mentally distance yourself from the thought. Why are you thinking this way?

- Then, replace it with a positive thought. Here's an example of changing your thoughts:

> ***In the past:*** *You don't agree with something the U.S. Senate has done. You rant and rave for hours about how stupid the legislators are. If it affected them, they'd sure think twice, and many other negative statements.*

> ***Revise your thinking:*** *The government has done something that angers you. Before you speak, you stop yourself and mentally step away from your emotions, which effectively shuts them down. Does this event drastically affect my life? My family? Is it that important in comparison to the universe? Of course, the answer is no. So, let it go.*

Keep the following in mind:

- Negative thoughts are our way of avoiding pain, which the ego avoids at all costs. So, confront and accept pain or negatives, then let them go and move on with your life ... preferably, to something more positive that gives you pleasure.

- The types of positive thoughts that empower you are: love, harmony, kindness, peace, joy, generosity, happiness and goodwill toward others.

- Allow the world to be as it is. Accept that it's suppose to be this way at this moment in time, and be positive about yourself and your life.

- Concern yourself only with those things you know you can change. The rest doesn't matter.

- The words *problem, failure and obstacle* are incorrect naming on your part. Problems and obstacles appear when you take your eyes off your goal; otherwise, you would see them as merely opportunities for growth and success. Failure is only a result and should be viewed as a milestone toward success.

Lee Iacocca, the once CEO of Chrysler, once said that if you haven't been fired from at least a few jobs, you haven't been trying hard enough to succeed. Then, he said to remember that at least "you" hadn't been fired from the position of voluntary chairman to renovate the Statue of Liberty — he was! You would believe that this is a great example of turning a negative into a positive, but it's not. Successful people don't see negatives. They only see opportunities for success. And in this instance, Iacocca took every firing to jump higher in his career.

- Affirmations are positive statements about yourself and your world. They are excellent for pushing the negative into Cold Storage. Use them as often each day as possible.

Self-Speech

Self-speech is an extension of negative thoughts and programming. Both contribute and cause negative self-speech. To remove it, you must change your attitude toward yourself and cultivate an inner voice that only supports and loves you.

As you remove your programming and change your negative thoughts to positive ones, you'll automatically begin to say less negative things about yourself; but remember, self-speech is a habit, too.
Change the habit by:

- Stop using labels to describe yourself. Stop referring to yourself as shy, American, fat, ugly, short, too tall, overweight, and so on. Labels place you in a very tiny box that is difficult to escape and cancels out who you really are. If you must use labels, then use only positive ones from this point on. You're assertive, outgoing, just the right weight, just the right height, attractive, and so on. Each time you catch yourself using a negative label, create a positive affirmation to repeat often and tape it up with the rest of them.

- Learn to love and respect yourself. Schedule one day each month with yourself. This means you plan to do something just for yourself and by yourself that pampers you and shows you love. If you live with others, do this outside the home to ensure your time with "you" is not interrupted. It could be a day at the spa, a day doing something you love to do, walking in the park — what would make you feel relaxed, self-love, and self-respect? Eventually, this love and respect for yourself will spill out to include how you feel about and treat others; and, since like energy attracts like energy, you'll receive love and respect from others. It doesn't happen overnight, but it will happen.

> "It is never too late to be
> what you might have been."
>
> George Eliot
>
> (aka: Mary Ann Evans)

Exercise

Exercise #7 — Reinvent Yourself

Now that you're thinking, speaking and reacting with an open mind, you're ready to determine.

- Taking the success goal you previously chose, imagine the ideal result of this goal. Imagine it in detail. Write it down in your journal. Take plenty of time.

- What will it take to achieve this goal? Write down everything in your journal. You may find that you need to do some research to write it all in detail.

- Put the "need to do's" in order of importance (the order always can be revised). Underline the most important ones and make these your milestones.

- Decide when you're going to start. Remember, starting may be researching topics and is seldom quitting your job and jumping into some venture. If research wasn't part of your to-do list, go back and revise it.

- Once you have a start date, create a plan of action and date the milestones. Give yourself some leeway in between, so you don't become single-minded in your quest.

It's important to balance your time to include your family, friends and the rest of your life.

Then, resolve to work on your goal each day. It doesn't have to be major efforts. Maybe, you will look for an article that is important to your goal. If you must miss a day or two because life has gotten in the way, don't worry. Just ensure you get back on your path to success as soon as possible.

Determination

Determination is making a statement of fact and following through on it. You declare yourself to be what it is you desire. You raise your ceiling of expectations for yourself and the world around you. You know that all things are possible, and you're capable of achieving this success. You're enthusiastic and passionate about yourself and your goal, so much that others feel it. You're at peace and happy. You know your purpose at this point in life. You take the necessary risks, knowing that they will move you toward your goal.

If you begin to experience obstacles, then you've taken your eyes off your goal. Refocus. Frustrated? You're off purpose. Refocus. Don't daydream about your success; just keep your focus on each step and milestone of your plan of action.

As your determination moves you toward your goal, you'll begin to see results manifest. Note these in your journal. Mark off your milestones once completed and celebrate each one.

Everything in this chapter helps you turn the internal negative energy into positive. The chapter entitled, "Trade-Offs", will help you with the external.

Give to Succeed

Charity is the key element in most religions, especially the six major world religions. The Bible mentions charity numerous times in the New Testament and offerings even more often in the Old Testament. Of Course, the Bible's Old Testament is a compilation of the Jewish Torah (The Law), Neviim (The Prophets), and Ketuvim (The Writings). Islam's sacred writing mentions the term charity throughout the Quran, especially in its first and longest Surah, *The Cow*. Though the word charity isn't used in Hindu writings, the premise of giving and aiding others is prevalent within the Rig Veda, Thirukkural, Bhagawad Gita, and other writings. Concerning charity in Buddhism, H.H. The Dalai Lama has stated, "... from the time of Buddha until today all forms of Buddhism have been continuously trying to help people, whether in social groups or individually ... The freedom and happiness of all living beings have always been the ultimate ideal and the working goal."[3] The sixth major world religion is Skihism, which carries a synthesized belief system from Islam and Hinduism.

---

[3] H.H. The Dalai Lama, *Buddhism in Practice*, Snow Lion Newsletter, Volume 11, Number 2, Snow Lion Publications, 1993.

Additionally, the Bible's Old Testament has several references to the word "sevenfold" and the phrase "seven times",[4] stating that what you put out through your actions (energy) comes back to you seven times stronger.

> *Genesis states in 4:15 & 24 that if Cain is slain, he'll be avenged sevenfold; the punishment for stealing is to pay what was stolen back sevenfold in Proverbs 6:31; and Isaiah 30:26 states that the sun shines seven times brighter than the moon.*

What these sacred texts are trying to impress upon us is how the universe responds to what we give — negatively or positively — in greater amounts.

It's better to give than to receive.

It's the way the universe works. It's a fundamental part of our lives.

When you seek success in anything, you have a tendency to focus totally on the goal and the process of getting there. That's a problem. The

[4] Terminology: Jones, Alexander (Editor), *The Jerusalem Bible*, Doubleday & Company, Inc., 1966.

more you chase after your own goals and pursue your self-interest, the more they elude you. When you're in a state of doing only for yourself, you are off your purpose.

Remember the previous discussion on the expansion of energy? What you have inside you, you radiate. What you give off, you attract to you. If you're focusing on your own self-interests, it's the same as being greedy. You're only concerned with receiving, which means you don't give. If you don't give, the universe doesn't give back to you. When you freely give only to help others without concern for what you'll receive in return, then the universe gives back to you in greater amounts. It's as simple as that.

You attract what you give, what's inside of you. If you give love, respect and empowerment, the universe returns what you radiate sevenfold. If you give of yourself in time and money, the universe returns your giving sevenfold.

Tammy is a single parent, who was having trouble making ends meet. She had been let go from her job and received no child support. Jobs were scarce and the rent was coming due. No matter what she did, she seemed to fail. The more she scrimped and worried, the worse her situation became. One day while visiting and keeping her mother company, they watched the 700 Club. There were a couple families on the show telling about how they were having serious financial problems. The people had seen the 700 Club's message about giving. Needless to say, Tammy decided to give ten percent of the little she had to the 700 Club's Operation Blessing and begin cherishing what she and her children had, rather than focusing on what they didn't have. Less than a week after giving to the charity, she found a job, allowing her to keep her apartment. She continued to give ten percent of her salary, regardless of her needs, and the universe continued to give to her in abundance. She now owns her own business and just purchased a new home.

We have heard many such stories like Tammy's. In each case, the people take the focus off themselves and their problems, give only for the purpose of giving and helping others, and receive sevenfold for their gift to the universe.

Did You Know?

In BusinessWeek's *Philanthropy 2004*[5], they reported the following:

Donor(s)	Position in Industry	Donation Amount	Charity
Bill & Melinda Gates	Microsoft founder	Est. $3 billion in MS dividends	Gates' charitable foundation, helping many charities
Gordon & Betty Moore	Co-Founder, Intel Corporation	$265 million/ 2/3 of wealth	Ocean research & training for nurses/ conservation & science
Alfred Mann	Medical device mogul	$200 million	Medical research
Sidney E. Frank	Liquor import king	$100 million	University scholarships
Stephen M. Ross	Related Cos., CEO	$100 million	A university school of business

[5] Conlin, Michelle, Gard, Lauren, and Hempel, Jessi with Hazelwood, Kate, Polek, David, and Fianco, Tony, Philanthropy 2004, BusinessWeek, McGraw-Hill Companies, Inc., November 29, 2004

Michael & Susan Dell	Dell Computers, Chairman of the Board	Almost $600 million	Children's causes
Ted Turner	Media Mogul	$1 billion	United Nations
Veronica Atkins	Widow of diet guru, Dr. Robert Atkins	$500 million	Diabetes & obesity
Oprah Winfrey	Talk show host and actress	Over $116 million	Education
Haim & Cheryl Saban	Founder, Chairman & CEO, Fox Family Worldwide	Over $116 million	Hospitals
William & Alice Goodwin	AMF Bowling Chairman	3/5 of their wealth	Cancer research & education
Pierre Omidyar	eBay founder	Over $116 million	Various charities types
James & Virginia Stowers, Jr.	American Century Cos. founder	2/3 of wealth	Medical research

Actress Angelia Jolie is the Goodwill Ambassador for the United Nations High Commissioner for Refugees and has spent millions of her own money to help in developing countries, as well as other charities.

Bono, lead singer of U2, has worked tirelessly to gather celebrities, politicians and government leaders to relieve the needless death of children in Africa through contributions, fund-raising, and forgiving debts owed by Africa to other nations. He gives both time and money to make a difference.

This list is only a fraction of the wealthy, which give both time and money to help others. This isn't a new trend. Over the years, many, who have inherited or obtained wealth, have donated large portions of their wealth to help others. The Rockefellers are an excellent example. By giving, they received more and kept what they already had.

Moving Toward Success

To move into the realm of purpose (the process of moving forward toward success), you must give and serve others. Focus on your goal in the NOW by continually working toward it without being "attached" to it. As soon as you attach emotion to the goal, it eludes you. Attach your emotion to helping others, and your success will chase after you.

Keep your giving to yourself. Otherwise, you cancel out its effect in the universe. If you're giving your time and resources for the right reason, you don't have a need to discuss it. The information on the philanthropists listed earlier came from public records. Though you know about Bono's works, which is necessary to gain more support, he never discloses how much he personally donates each year.

So, give of time and money to succeed.

Exercises

Exercise #8 — Plan of Action

- Copy the table on page 50.

- In the first column, list the charities that you currently support financially. Include amounts, frequency and the charity. For example:

$100 monthly, St Jude's Children's Hospital.

- In the second column, make a list of all that you currently do in time and effort to aid and support charities and those in need. Include the amount of time, what it is you do, frequency, the charity, and how it helps. Example:

2 hrs, weekly, local food pantry, helps homeless/ poor.

- In the third and fourth columns, list what additional things you would like to do now and in the future.

- Later chapters in this book will help you free up more of your time. Remember, giving of time can be a family project.

    When John's children were preteens and teens, he and his wife did a lot of volunteering for charity in which their children could help. Here are just two of the projects, where their children received lessons that would take them through adulthood: They taught English to third-world families, new to the United States, who were sponsored by their church. The children helped with John's work for a political campaign — delivering pamphlets door-to-door and working in the campaign headquarters while he made calls to party members.

    Just think what working in a soup kitchen or a food pantry would do to help your own children better appreciate what they have.

- There are two methods that people use to determine how much to give financially: The first is to start with a comfortable amount, and then double it. The second (and most popular) is to just use the ten percent of income rule. Ten percent is the minimum you should be giving. If you feel like giving more, do so.

- Now, use these two last columns as goals to achieve and start working toward them. (Financially, the ten percent should be done immediately to a worthwhile charity. Anything above and beyond the ten percent is your goal to work toward.)

Current Charitable Efforts		Planned Charitable Efforts	
Financially	Time & Effort	Financially	Time & Effort

Silence Your Mind

The world of silence. It's a place to explore who you truly are, to create, and to connect to the universe. In the silence, you connect to love. In the silence, you access the power of the universe. It clears your mind and gives you extraordinary ideas, allowing success to flow freely.

The silence is within that part of yourself that *No One Knows*, where you may encounter the true purpose of your life and what you need do to achieve it. In the silence, you recharge your batteries, remove tension and anxiety, reduce stress and fatigue, eliminate doubt and depression, and remove enculturation programming. It gives you a sense of belonging. You become one with the universe and all of humanity, and you know peace.

When you are separated from the silence, you see doubts, your see problems, and you feel the negative surround you. There are no problems, doubts or negative in the silence. It moves you away from this outer world and all its perceived troubles, connecting you back to your original source of spirit.

This silence is located in the space between your thoughts. To reach it, you must quiet your thoughts. You must quiet your mind and know stillness. Then, you merge with it.

The gateway to silence, this space between your thoughts, is meditation, of which there are many forms. Some people believe that meditation is only a form of worship in Buddhism, but even Christianity has a practiced form of meditation — members of the Roman Catholic Church pray the Rosary, and prayer, itself, is a form of meditation.

The important thing is to quiet your mind, be at peace, and connect.

Take a walk in the woods or a quiet park. Listen to the sounds of nature. Breathe deeply of the fresh air. Hear the birds chirping, the leaves rustling under foot, and the sound and smell of the breeze as it brushes past your face. Walk barefoot in the grass. Stretch your arms out wide and slowly turn, feeling the freedom. Feel the different textures of nature — the bark of a tree, the silky feel of a flower petal, the soft fur of a kitten, the bristles from the blades of grass against you palm, and all that nature offers your senses. As you focus on hearing and feeling nature, you will find peace.

While you're alone, speak to the universe — in your mind through your thoughts or out loud, depending upon your comfort level. Speak as if you're speaking to a friend. Tell this friend your problems and desires. Then, let the universe take care of them.

Singing or playing an instrument during this time may bring you closer to your source, depending upon the music produced.

> *Patricia plays the Native American flute (NAF). It's a 23½-inch long, cedar, hand-carved flute in the key of G. She can use sheet music, but the NAF is created to play from the music that comes from within her. Patricia just plays from her soul and spirit. This particular flute produces a low, soulful, almost haunting sound. If anyone passes by, she never knows it — they usually just quietly sit and listen. Regardless of where she's at, playing the*

NAF definitely brings Patricia closer to the universe, as well as anyone in listening distance. It's healing and uplifting.

You should plan to commune with nature on a regular basis. Put it in your schedule. At least one full day a month should be devoted to it. You could combine this day with the "being good to yourself" day, discussed earlier.

Another meditation form is to mentally review in your mind something that is unresolved or causing you problems three-to-five minutes before falling to sleep. Imagine the situation being resolved in a positive manner, and ask your subconscious (the universe) to resolve the issue, with you knowing what to do upon waking. Write in your journal the next morning, before leaving your bed. Continue to write until you see a response to your request.

To really see results faster use a more formal, deeper method of meditation, one that you practice on a daily basis.

Deep Meditation Technique

There are several methods of deep meditation. Here's the one that always has works well for beginners:

1. Set aside time in a quiet place, where you will not be disturbed. Place your journal and a pen/pencil close at hand. When you first begin meditating, you may prefer a darkened room, using a candle to keep your focus. Some people envision a bright star in their minds, but this is a bit more difficult to hold constant.

2. You may wish to add music to "jump start" your meditation in order to elevate your connection to the universe and control your

thoughts. With practice, train your mind to continue meditating at the higher level, after the music stops. We suggest any music CD by R. Carlos Nakai (a uniquely-talented Native American flutist), any of the "Celtic Twilight" music CDs (several different volumes are available on Amazon.com), any other similar music. You even may prefer to use one piece of music (with or without words) that immediately connects you to the universe at the level of your soul and spirit. You'll know if it does this, because it will bring tears to your eyes and a swelling in your chest; yet once you connect to your source, you are awash with happiness and peace like you've never before felt. Two such songs that do this for a colleague are: "I Want to Know" (long version), by Foreigner, and "Yeshua Ha Mashiach" (translated means Jesus the Messiah), by Scott Wesley Brown (from "The Scott Wesley Brown Collection"). Both may be found on Amazon.com.

3. Set comfortably but alertly in a comfortable chair or on a pillow on the floor. You may lie in bed in the morning after waking or at

night before sleeping; but it's very easy to
fall asleep.

4. Focus on the candle flame, empty your
   mind, and still your body. At first, you will
   find your mind taking control and
   wondering all over the place. This is
   normal. When you realize that your mind
   is wondering out of control, just refocus on
   the candle flame and empty your mind
   again. It takes practice over time to be able
   to keep your mind blank for any length of
   time. Focus until you're no longer aware of
   your physical body.

5. Once you have your focus, you have many
   choices of what to do next:

   a. Be still and let God). Just allow the
      universe to merge with you, letting
      you feel its presence. You may do an
      entire meditation like this, if you
      wish.

   b. Use a mantra, especially helpful at
      first. It keeps your attention on your
      source, controlling your wandering

thoughts. Some individuals and religions believe a mantra connects with evil or pagan spirits, but this is not true. We suggest two mantras, if you so choose to use one:

i. Repeat the word, "Om". Om and the use of mantras originate from Vedic Hinduism, later adopted by Buddhists and Jains. In the Bible, John 1:1 states, "In the beginning was the Word: the Word was with God and the Word was God." In Vedic Hinduism, Om is that "Word", the vibration that set the creation of the world in motion. Chanting Om is said to correspond to that original vibration, connecting you back to your source. Om is pronounced A – U – M, accenting each syllable. Here's how it connects you: "A" is where you are current in a waking state; "U" takes you to a state similar to the dream state, and "M" to the state similar to deep sleep. The silence between the syllables is the state of perfect bliss — your connection to the universe — and is achieved by the repetition of Om. With practice, this mantra takes you to your source, the silence between the syllables, the space between your thoughts.

ii. Another mantra method is used in Japa Meditation, where the name of God is repeated while focusing on your intentions. It works well, especially if you are having a difficult time shutting out the day-to-day thoughts that dominate your mind. There are many names for God in the Bible; and you can research all of the Hebrew names (as well as in other faiths) for God and choose one of them — whichever name for God that has meaning for you.

c. Conversing with the universe within your mind is another choice. Don't ask for things or pass along information here. The universe already knows the needs and desires of yourself and everyone else in the world.

This is the time to turn over your problems and concerns to the universe, then make an affirmation statement. For example:

> **Problem***: "I am concerned about meeting my financial responsibilities".*

> **Affirmation***: "I know my needs are already provided by you, and I am not concerned."*

d. Then, be still in the silence and listen for the response. As to what type of response you receive will depend upon your proficiency in meditation. You may *hear* a *voice* (thoughts that aren't your own) in your mind that speaks to you, or you may see pictures/video (visions) in your mind.

On the last day of a religious workshop, a participant stated that he had prayed the Rosary daily for many years. All he ever asked for was to hear the voice of God. It was evident during his explanation that this was very upsetting for him. The priest giving the workshop didn't have an answer for him, nor did anyone else. When the class had ended, Howard (another participant) went to the man, who was still sitting, and knelt next to him. Some people held back to see what Howard would say, expecting to possibly join him in praying with the distraught man.

Instead, Howard asked him, "When you pray the Rosary, what do you see in your mind?"

Surprised at the question, the man answered, "The face of the Virgin Mary. She's always smiling."

"And do you have a particular devotion to the Virgin Mary?"

"Yes, I do. Why?" asked the man, who now was curious.

Howard broke into a wide smile and said, "This is God's way of saying 'hello' to you!"

The man broke down in tears, as did many around him.

After he composed himself, Howard explained that it takes truly knowing yourself inside and out to be able to differentiate your thought patterns from the "voice" of God. Therefore, God usually begins speaking to you in pictures. For this man, God *used something very special to him to let him know He was there and listening.*

Once you have this first awareness that the universe is responding to you, you'll begin to get many more pictures (visions). So, pay attention to what you "see" within your mind during your meditation. Sometimes, the visions move so fast and there are so many that you can't remember them all after the meditation, but let them flow. Once you begin trying to remember, you engage your brain and the visions stop. Just pay close attention to what you "see".

e. Be sure to thank your source, not only for this time/response but also for all it provides to you.

After the meditation is over, immediately write down any experiences you had in your journal. Don't worry if you didn't feel that you had a "good" meditation — there is no such thing as a bad one. Something is accomplished at all meditations, whether you are aware of it or not. Just keep at it and observe all the mental pictures and "chatter"; then, write everything you remember in your journal. Eventually, you'll see responses and/or patterns emerge.

Keep your experiences to yourself, especially in the beginning. Otherwise, you may find yourself having to explain and defend ideas and insights you were given. Then, the ego has entered and manifesting (the universe-driven process) stops.

Exercises

Exercise #9 — Meditation

Begin doing a meditation daily, using the deep technique outlined previously. With at least 20 minutes a day, continue meditating for at least two months. Once you are comfortable meditating, begin to focus it on your chosen success.

Exercise #10 — Additional Connections

Chose one other method of connecting to the universe (presented before the deep meditation technique) to do at least once monthly, though weekly provides you a continual sense of peace. Write these experiences in your journal.

Believe It Now!

In the first chapter, we mentioned that success takes both determination and belief. This requires a belief that is with absolute certainty that your goal already has taken place in the universe. It only needs be manifest — made real in the physical world — exactly on time. Believing with absolute certainty is a giant "leap of faith" that the universe will come through for you.

One of the strongest tools for keeping your proper focus is, of course, meditation, because it connects you directly to the universe and affirms your faith in it. An even stronger tool is to actually see the universe in motion — seeing things happen for you without any intervention from you, other than determination and belief.

Once, Julie and her mother were going to a fairly large mall during the Christmas season. Of course, the parking lot was packed with shoppers. Julie began to drive toward the front of the parking lot, by the main doors of the mall out of habit. Her mother asked her what she was doing, and

Julie told her mother that she wanted to see if there were any empty spots close to the front doors. Her mother very indignantly told Julie that she was crazy. Julie's response? "Oh ye of little faith!" and silently asked God if He might provide a spot close for her mother to see that things are possible through belief. Julie was as shocked as her mother, when there was a newly-vacated spot directly in front of the doors in the first position. Julie pulled in the space without a word said, while her young children began giggling in the back seat. After shutting off the car, she turned to her mother and said, "God provides." Then, silently thanked Him. It took a while for her mother to recover from the shock. Julie has since asked God for close parking spots many times, knowing that if there isn't one, it's because someone with a greater need got it. More times than not, the space is there. Oh, and Julie's mother's faith in the universe grew that day by leaps and bounds.

Did Julie know for sure a space would be there? No, but she did absolutely believe that her prayer was heard and would be positively answered, if at all possible within the current circumstances of her life. That is belief from determination. You first determine, and then follow it with absolute belief.

Notice also that Julie asked for a space "close" to the doors. She didn't limit the universe by asking for a specific space. She allowed the universe room to process her request.

> *Let's say, instead of someone having just pulled out of the first space, they had just pulled out of one five spaces down. If Julie had asked specifically for the first space, then the space five spaces down may have been given to someone else. She would have been trying to manipulate the process.*

You must not limit the result of your request. Allow the universe to define the best outcome. The source knows better than we do the best result for us at the moment in time it manifests into our physical world.

Be the Success You Desire

Another important factor in absolute belief is treating yourself as if and acting as though your goal is already achieved. Remember, that as soon as you determine something and place absolute belief in it, it already has been processed by the universe and exists — even if the existence is currently in thought. Don't think about what has been, the past is gone. Treat the situation as if the past had never happened. Change the way you look at the situation to a positive perspective. Think, speak and act/react with a sense of purpose. Have gratitude for the universe, yourself and the situation, and be inspired.

Let's look at some examples:

> **Example 1:** *You wish to shed enough weight before an important function to fit in to a new dress. You have determined that you will lose the weight and have, in fact, already lost the weight in thought within the universe. You believe with absolute certainty that the universe is processing your request by moving the world's energy to accommodate you.*

Do you continue eating as if it doesn't matter? Do you continue being a couch potato? That would say that your goal doesn't matter and would effectively stop the process. If you look in the mirror and are repulsed or constantly use the overweight or fat words in your thoughts and spoken words, wanting to be thin, then you'll retain the 20 pounds, no matter what you do.

Instead, you outline what needs to be done to get to where you wish to be. That would include eating and exercising properly. You compliment yourself on your thin and shapely figure and how your clothes fit so perfectly each time you look in the mirror. You love and appreciate yourself.

Yes, the proper eating and exercise will help you lose

weight, by the sheer fact that you're doing them. But they won't ensure you lose enough weight to fit in that new dress on time, let alone look perfect; and maybe, you only needed to lose 15 pounds. The universe will take care of the amount of weight. You take care of treating yourself and acting as if it's already happened, because it has.

Example 2: *Your marriage is in constant conflict. You spouse starts fighting over the littlest details, any excuse to yell and scream at you. You determine that your marriage is going to be harmonious and believe with absolute certainty that the universe has made it so.*

Again, you must act as if it is so. You act in harmony, regardless of what your spouse does. You remain positive and don't allow your mate to affect your peace.

You smile a lot. Surprise him with a hug and kiss him on the cheek, when he begins a fight; then, change the subject to something pleasant or leave to do something in another room. You always remain in peace and harmony in your thoughts, speech and actions/reactions. Now, obviously, this in itself will affect your spouse; and you may subconsciously stop doing things that irritate your mate.

Let's say, however, you aren't doing anything to irritate the spouse and he is starting the fights because of his own infidelity, creating an excuse (the bad marriage) for his unfaithful actions. No amount of peace and harmony on your part, alone, would change the situation. The universe, however, can do the impossible, by changing the spouse's perspective on both his marriage, you and his infidelity.

Or the universe may give you a harmonious marriage with a different spouse (so, ensure your determination is correctly stated). So, your actions of determination, absolute belief, and conducting yourself as if everything already has changed allows the universe to set in motion the forces that will collaborate with you to make your success manifest in the physical world.

Lastly, check every conscious thought, word and action against your goal. Does it match up with you plan for success? Or is it a hindrance? Match your perspective to your plan of action.

NOTE: A positive byproduct of absolute belief is that you develop more tolerance for the beliefs of others, adding more positive into your life. Once you have enough faith in your own beliefs, it's nearly impossible to be offended at the thoughts of others. You may even find them interesting.

Exercises

Exercise #11 — What's Important?

Review Exercise #6. Look at the things you've been doing, saying, and thinking. Looking at your plan of action, how may these things affect your success? Other than what you're already working on from previous exercises, what changes about yourself should you change in order to see that success manifest itself in your life? Make a list of all these things, and begin making the changes one item at a time.

Exercise #12 — Wanting to Believing

Review again your plan of action and its steps and milestones. Can you revise these to be more "believe it now", rather than "wanting"? If yes, then revise them to be absolute certainties.

Become Inspired

Along with determination and belief is being enthusiastic about your goal. Everything that happens along the way is another joyous milestone, moving you another step closer to success. Enthusiasm adds to your positive perspective and affirms your belief in the outcome.

Enthusiasm comes from inspiration. Inspiration comes from knowledge and enrichment of the mind, while ignorance fosters and intensifies fear. Inspiration also helps you to further define and detail your plan of action.

Inspiration may be obtained through many sources. The most obvious is education, whether it is motivational material to keep you on your path or gaining more specific knowledge to achieve your success. Education may be reading books, magazines, and journals, taking workshops and classes, listening to tapes/CDs, and watching videos that educate and motivate in the area of your goal. You become what you study, so expose your mind to anything and everything that adds to the achievement of your success.

Also, include educational and motivational materials that will help you after your success is achieved. Currently, you are in "the process". Once you've achieved your goal, you need to already have the knowledge and motivation to use the success in a positive manner and keep it moving forward.

Power of Association

The people that surround you influence your path, your attitude, your determination, your belief, your inspiration, and the outcome of your success. You should surround yourself with people who share your positive vision and desire to achieve your goal. Otherwise, you may be eliminating your success through the power of association.

Associations may mean being around the people who can make your success happen. Donald Trump did just this. He associated with those people, whom he wanted to emulate and who could assist his success.

Now, you may not desire that type of success; however, associations still impact your goals. Let me give you an example.

> *Darren used to be an alcoholic. After he hit bottom, he went into rehab and cleaned up his life. He joined Alcoholics Anonymous (AA) and tried to convince his wife to join Al-Anon, an arm of AA that helps spouses of alcoholics to eliminate all of their "old habits" they developed over the years to cope with the alcoholism (however, they also trigger a recovering alcoholic's past habits, as well). She refused any type of counseling and, at every opportunity, would "push Darren's buttons". Having difficulty retaining his sobriety under his wife's subconscious attempts to return to her comfort zone (though it was detrimental to her well-being, since Darren was physically abusive when drunk), Darren*

eventually divorced his wife. He's now been sober and happily remarried to a supporting spouse for many years.

Need for Heroes

One of the most supporting and inspirational tools to achieve success is to have a hero. Oprah Winfrey, talk show host, once told Barbara Walters, renowned interviewer and newscaster, that, if it were not for Ms. Walters, she wouldn't be where she is today. This is a wonderful example of using a hero to achieve. The great thing about emulating heroes is that they can be living, dead or even fictitious.

Finding a hero (or heroine) to emulate gives you many achievement advantages. That person is already the success you seek. Learn all you can about them. If possible, take them to lunch and interview them. Find out what they purposefully did to achieve. What could they have done differently to make the process to success easier and faster? Put photos of this individual all over your living space and on your desk at work. Keep a list of the person's traits that you wish to emulate, and incorporate them and anything that helped your hero to achieve into your plan of action.

Exercises

Exercise #13 — Education and Motivation

Using the library and the Internet, research to locate materials that will help you achieve your success. If you need more information and details (for instance, you would like to take a particular type of course in your area), research whatever resources necessary (for example: telephoning your local colleges for information on available classes). Incorporate these materials into your plan of action (i.e., reading material, taking classes, and so on). Then, be vigilant about placing as much priority on these plan items, as you would any other step to success.

Exercise #14 — Power of Association

Are the people who surround you holding you back? Evaluate your relationships against your chosen success. Are there any associations that are detrimental to achieving your goal? Make a list of possible problem individuals; then, turn it over to the universe during meditation. Ask for guidance on what you should do. You may be told that the individual is contributing to your success in a more important manner than what you see.

There are many possible solutions to a situation, other than discontinuing the relationship. Be sure to keep notes in your journal.

Exercise #15 — Heroes

If you don't already have one, find a hero, who is successful in your chosen goal area. Then, do all the things suggested in the earlier paragraph, entitled "Need for Heroes". Keep notes in your journal.

Trade-Offs

Returning again to the graphic of the human brain on page 36, let's look at how our activities may cause negativity. There are many ways in which we entertain and work our minds. Often, we choose activities that cause barriers to our success by adding a continuous stream of negativity into our brains' storehouse, rather than enriching our lives.

News Sources. How many different forms of the news do you see and/or hear each day? It comes by way of the radio, television, the newspaper, magazines, and the Internet via our computers. There are clipping services dedicated to providing specific types of news by email or mail.

Exercise

Exercise #16 — Your Newspaper

Take a copy of your local, daily newspaper. Any day will do. Get a black and a red magic marker. Do the following:

- Using the black magic marker and the front page only, outline and X through anything that is negative. This would include the weather that's generally in an upper corner, if the report isn't a positive forecast.

- Now, take the red marker and outline and X through the remaining verbiage. It has to be positive information/news, or it would already be marked in black.

How much red do you see, as compared to black? (Our experience with this exercise has been that there's very little red.) Now, envision multiplying the amount of black, which is the negative, times the number of pages in the newspaper; and then times the number of newspapers you read each day.

That's how much negative you are placing in your brain's storage each day just from newspapers.

You can further compound the news in the newspaper by each time you listen to the news on the radio, even those short briefs every hour. Then, add in each news magazine and journal you read each month. Now, include the television news you watch — don't forget the noon news, the nightly news, and the end of the day news programs, each are at least 30 minutes in length. How about the news shows — 60 Minutes, Meet the Press, Dateline NBC, The Today Show, and Good Morning America, just to name a few. Don't forget the totally news cable channels — Fox, CNN, MSNBC, and so on. Then, there are the Internet news sites, web sites with news feeds on them, and news emails delivered to your inbox.

Your last exercise shows how much of the news is negative. How can you replace negative thoughts in storage with positive, when you bombard your senses with all this negativity on a daily basis. Do you really need to see and hear all this news?

Choose one form, once a day, and eliminate all the rest. For instance, only the nightly news that gives a brief accounting without all the details. The addition of images and brief interviews are like a picture — they are worth a thousand words.

You get more in less time, without going in depth. You're also getting the headlines, which concerns you the most. You don't have to know about every problem across the world, in your state, city and neighborhood, or every little gruesome detail about a local murder.

Other Negative Sources. What type of books and magazines do you read? What type of movies and videos do you watch? Do you play electronic/ Internet games? What television shows do you watch?

Constantly reading and seeing violent media adds additional negativity. Consider this: you love the forensic and justice television shows — NCIS; all the CSI shows; all the Law and Order shows; the forensic shows on the Discovery channel, the History channel, and the Arts & Entertainment channel; NUMB3RS; and Bones. This is just a portion of the forensic and justice shows on the television schedule this season. If you're watching them all or even a good portion of them, look at all the negative you're putting into your mind. Like the news, you don't have to get rid of all of them. You could, for instance, choose to watch NCIS, the one CSI show you like the best, and NUMB3RS. Replace the other shows with positive, uplifting shows, or spend more time doing other activities. Also, be aware of the negativity given off by the "reality" shows.

To what music do you listen? How much alcohol and medication (or other drugs) do you ingest? How much caffeine do you intake? What type of things do you have in your home? On your walls? In your office? On your office desk? Do these things and activities energize you? Do they soothe you? Are your habits healthy? If your answer is no, then they are adding negative energy into you mind and body, contributing to stress and negative feelings. Again, replace what is negative with positive alternatives. These are all trade-offs you make for a better and more positive life.

Physical Comforts. One of the most difficult trade-offs is physical comforts. Many people never achieve their success, because they are not willing to "give up" anything in order to achieve their dream.

In the book, entitled "Rich Dad, Poor Dad"[6], Robert T. Kiyosaki tells of the poor dad, who worked hard in a job to earn and borrow money for that nice home, car and what luxuries his meager salary afforded him. Whereas, the rich dad provided for his family's necessities, never borrowed, and put every cent he had into his business (his dream). He had his family onboard with him, and it seemed they had a wealth of love and togetherness. They also had a back porch, screen door that was in sad need of repair for many years. The poor dad would have fixed it immediately; whereas, the rich dad felt the door still worked and the money to fix it served his family better being reinvested into the business. The poor dad remained in the same financial situation his entire life and continued to dream of being rich. The rich dad eventually moved his family into luxury and wealth.

Another example of trade-offs to achieve success is Jess P. Lair, Ph.D. In his book,

---

[6] Kiyosaki, Robert T. with Lechter, Sharon L., *Rich Dad, Poor Dad: What the rich teach their kids about money – that the poor and middle class do not!* Warner Books, 1998.

entitled "I Ain't Much Baby – But I'm All I've Got"[7], he shares his success of finding himself and his true purpose in life. He was in advertising and doing quite well financially. He was successful but overworked and stressed out. He got a chance to evaluate how unhappy he was, while being wheeled into surgery for a heart attack, and remembered his dream of being a college professor. After he healed, he sat his family down and told them what he wanted to do. His family agreed, with reservations but with love for him. He sold his advertising agency and their luxurious home, and they moved to a farm (the other part of his dream). He enrolled in a nearby college. In the early '90s, when Dr. Lair wrote the book, he was a college professor. He has since written many other books.

Both of the above are excellent examples of people who temporarily traded off their comfort for success. Most people aren't willing to do this because of fear and greed, which keeps them living paycheck to paycheck, barely earning

---

[7] Lair Ph.D., Jess P., *I Ain't Much Baby – But I'm All I've Got*. Fawcett Books, 1990, reissue 1995.

enough to keep up with their spending, and slaves to money and their material possessions.

Do you really need the big house in the fancy neighborhood? Or could an apartment in another neighborhood, which costs less, do just as well? Do you need the large salary you currently make at a job that doesn't contribute to your goal? Or can you make trade-offs in your lifestyle to allow yourself to take that job that will lead you to success?

We have bought into the *American Dream* of owning our own home, driving an upscale car, and constantly spending to get more. The advertising industry pays its creative minds lots of money to continue to sell you on this *Dream*. You must shut off such messages that continually surround and bombard you. Learn to live by the "beat of your own drum."

Exercises

Exercise #17 — Lessening the Negative

- Make several copies of the "Eliminating Negativity" table on page 77.

- For the next week, list in the table all the sources of news you see and/or hear, as well as other sources of negativity. Review this chapter each day to ensure you're locating as much of these negative sources as possible.

- At the end of the week, review the table's news column. Create a plan of action by first eliminating as many news sources as possible. For example: Choose only one daily news source, such as the nightly news. Write "nightly news" in the plan of action, news column. Then, take a red pen and put one line through all the others in the first column to remind yourself that you will never watch, listen or read these again.

- Now, look at the other negative sources listed in column two. For all negative media, either eliminate them, choose only one or two, and/or substitute alternatives. For video gaming, either eliminate them all or choose only one and limit your playing time. For furnishings you have a negative feel about, burn dried sage to rid each room of negativity as the Native Americans do and use Feng Shui for furniture and item arrangements — or just replace the items. For all other items, such as alcohol, diet and drugs, use alternatives, elimination or reduction for positive results.

- Next, follow through on your plan of action. That may mean creating affirmations that are taped to the television set(s) and other such reminders

Exercise #18 — Comfort Trade-Offs

- Make several copies of the "Trade-Off" table on page 78.

- In the first column, list all the things you currently have or do that could be eliminated or substituted with alternatives AND, by doing so, would assist you to achieve your success — whether they are plausible or not.

- In column two, list what you would substitute for the items in column one. For example, the occasional concert and movies for the current civic center season tickets. A nice apartment, where someone else pays for the upkeep inside and out, for the two-story home that takes a lot of upkeep in both time and money. To create more harmony in your marriage, forego the weekly boys' night out; instead, go only once a month and spend the other three nights doing something special with your wife. Look for positive alternatives.

- Now, create a plan of action, which may include discussing the idea with your spouse and anyone else the change may affect. Revise your plan of action as needed. Remember, not to create more change at one time than you and others are able to handle effectively.

Eliminating Negativity Table

Negative Repetition		Plan of Action	
News	Other Sources	News	Other Sources

Trade-Off Table

Current Situation	Possible Alternatives	Plan of Action

Success from Chaos

The mind requires a balance between work and leisure activities. You need to feel pleasure, challenge, reward, failure (in order to appreciate success), and so on. Unfortunately, we feed our minds very poorly. In the last decade, workaholics abound, with people working two and three jobs just to make ends meet, or 60 to 80 hours every week for fear of losing your job if you don't.

You need to gain a new perspective on the needs of the mind — it needs to be exercised vigorously (work) and relaxed often (leisure activities and rest), just like a muscle in the body. Too much work causes your mind to produce stress and fatigue, regardless of how much sleep you get. Too much leisure, your mind produces depression and apathy. It's easy to see why an imbalance is detrimental to achieving your success.

A balance allows your mind to function at peak performance, including that Johari Window Quadrant that No One Knows, the area that you go to between your thoughts during meditation. A balanced life allows you to more easily connect to the universe, the core element in achieving your success.

The key to achieving a balanced lifestyle is to eliminate chaos from your life. Chaos not only takes up time in your physical life, it takes up mental time and capacity. Chaos is the element that generally induces stress. It causes sleepless nights and interferes with meditation. It keeps your mind moving a mile a minute.

Eliminating chaos from your life and achieving balance eliminates stress and mental fatigue, allowing you to focus on important things. It gives you the freedom to create, a necessary element of success. Another great thing about eliminating chaos is that it frees up time that may be used in other endeavors, including working toward your success. How do you eliminate chaos? By simplifying your life. Clutter causes chaos. Get rid of clutter, and you simplify your life.

Eliminating Chaos at Work

When you simplify your work life, you work smarter, have more time to do what's important, and work less hours. Though your work situation is different from anyone else's, here are a few ideas to consider for simplifying your life and reducing or eliminating chaos, clutter and stress:

- Work less hours by working more efficiently. If you're working all the time, you have no time to be still, allowing your mind to think or create successfully.

- Schedule time (or just take it when necessary) to be still in order to clear your head and allow the "creative juices" to flow. You'll find that ideas and solutions formulate much easier and faster.

- Use time more efficiently. Clean your desk at the end of each day and put away papers and files. Create a to-do list, too. The next workday, you're ready to start fresh, can find everything you need, and know where to begin working immediately. All you need do is get your coffee and get started.

- Take your vacations and stay home when you're ill. You do not work effectively or efficiently, when you are fatigued or not up to par. Plus, you give your illness to others at work, costing the company in more lost production than just your one or two days sick leave. Vacations rejuvenate you, if planned correctly (don't wear yourself out doing more than time allows or working at home the whole time — do something fun and relaxing).

- Consider the different work alternatives (against your chosen success): full time, part time, telecommuting, don't work, flex time, or working for yourself at home.

- How about a different job or different line of work to accommodate or add to your success.

- You may need to simplify your work life by finding another job with a worker-friendly environment.

- For all meetings, always ask, "Do I really need to do this?" Avoid needless meetings that drain time and energy.

- Minimize the number of lunch dates and work-related gatherings (either during or outside of work). Take your lunch every day and do something relaxing. Don't work through lunch, and don't eat at your desk.

- Give yourself a break each morning and afternoon, even if only to get your own coffee. Take a couple minutes to chat with co-workers (but don't overdo it). Write the breaks "inconspicuously" into your schedule, or use your computer's calendar alarm and label it CB for coffee break.

- Take an occasional pause and breathe deeply; stand up and stretch. It's easy to work for over four hours without realizing it. Use that computer calendar alarm to alert you periodically throughout the day.

- Eliminate distractions. Do your personal business at home, including personal telephone calls and emails. Minimize co-worker socializing. If you have a secretary, have him/her screen your visitors. Stand when someone enters your office — invite those you need to do business with to sit; all others, continue standing, and (after they have a quick say) let them know you're on deadline and would love to talk later, hinting that it's time for them to leave.

- Manage the people you work for, with and supervise by setting boundaries. Never automatically say yes. Don't accept unreasonable requests or problems from others — let them solve them or, at least, bring you a reasonable solution. If you don't have a quick answer for someone requesting something unreasonable, say, "Let me think about that, and I'll get back to you."

- Manage your workload. Many people do more than their boss expects, either thinking they have to or that it will impress the boss. Eighty percent of your boss' satisfaction is related to only 20 percent of your work performance. That means you should focus 80% of your time on that 20% of work. If necessary, ask your boss what's important to him for you to accomplish.

- Don't make promises you cannot keep, especially meeting impossible deadlines.

- If you get overwhelmed at work, stop and leave your desk for a few minutes. Walk around the block or up/down a flight of stairs, or go for coffee. Breathe deeply and relax your mind. If frustrated, laugh out loud until your body relaxes and your feel refreshed.

- Don't procrastinate. Handle a piece of paper only once, whenever possible. You'll find the work flows more smoothly, there's less frustrations, and your inbox gets cleared faster.

- Take the path of least resistance that still satisfies the situation.

- Cut down on the paper. Take your name off "nice to have" routing lists. Cancel any subscriptions (including those through the Internet and email) that aren't absolutely necessary (magazines, business reports, and so on). If you have a secretary or assistant, train him/her to read any media you need and highlight important information for you.

- Reduce the business junk mail that robs you of time and energy[8]. Send personal mail to your home address, and work mail to your work address. Whenever you order anything or make charitable donations, request that your information not be sold or passed on to anyone else.

- Eliminate email overload. Be selective about giving out your email address. Don't put it on your business card. Ask to be deleted from email mailing lists. Keep a Hotmail or Yahoo mail account to use when signing up for anything on the Internet. Keep your emails focused only on work. Ask co-workers to keep emails short and for business only. Turn off the beep that announces each new email. Schedule email checking periodically, using your computer calendar alarm. Unsubscribe to spam or ask your IT person to catch it at the server and report it to the appropriate Internet

---

[8] Go to www.metrokc.gov/dnrp/swd/nwpc/bizjunkmail.htm for resources to get your name off mail lists. Do a search for "reduce junk mail" (in quotes) for other resources. Call 1-888-5OptOut to request Equifax, Trans Union, Novas and Experian not use your name for credit card offers. On junk mail you receive, call the 800 number they provide and request to be taken off their list and not to sell it to anyone else.

abuse web sites (they can get this information from your company's isp).

- Cut down on your telephone time. Don't give out your cell phone or beeper number at work, and don't have them printed on your business card. If you use your cell phone for both home and business and must give someone, including a client, an alternative contact number, use a beeper number (otherwise, they will continue to use your cell number, even when you're away from work). If your company supplies your cell phone for business use, you will have a harder time eliminating this time consumer.

Have your secretary or assistant screen your calls and take messages. Just like emails, schedule time to listen to telephone messages and do call backs periodically during the day. Don't play telephone tag, use voicemail and leave messages.

Eliminating Chaos at Home

If you review the listed items above, many translate effectively to your home life.

- Do you schedule "think" time? How about not trying to do everything in one day?

- Are you always on the run? Must each of your children participate in five different activities each week? Can you combine errands together? Shop only once weekly or every two weeks, rather than daily? What else can you eliminate or reduce?

- Leave your briefcase at work. Don't bring it home, and don't work overtime (especially, weekends). Work shouldn't cut into your leisure time, especially when you have a family. (Many workaholics work to avoid these relationships; or they believe they must continue to provide "more" for the family, who would much prefer the person at home.)

- All those fix-it chores — what about hiring neighboring teens to do them? Or a professional service for the lawn care and snow removal?

- Take the path of least resistance that still satisfies the situation.

- Develop a quality home life. Do fun things with family and friends.

- Cultivate new friendships and interests.

- Screen phone calls at home. Use a message machine or the telephone company's voice messaging. Eliminate call waiting telephone features — always know who is on the other end of the line before answering. Don't feel that you need to speak to every person that calls. Leave call backs to convenient times. No matter how upsetting, never take business calls at home, unless a case of life or death. Handle all business during work hours.

- Turn off the cell phone, when enjoying leisure activities. It's not only annoying to other people, but it stops the flow of creativity and relaxation of the mind.

- Get rid of junk mail. See the work section on this.

- Control your email and spam. See the work section on this.

- Cut down on your television time. Do activities that are more pleasurable. Spend time with your family.

Exercise

Exercise #19 — Cut the Chaos

- Make several copies of the following table.

- Using a different table for work and home, do the following for each.

- In column one, list all the events or situations that take up your time, especially if they use a lot of it or cause energy drains.

- In column two, list for each item in column one what you might do to change the situation. Like the examples in this chapter, what alternatives might you put in place to get rid of the clutter and chaos?

- In column three, make a plan of action and do it.

Current Situation	Possible Alternatives	Plan of Action

In Summary

Achieving success won't necessarily happen overnight; however, by properly using the skills given you in this book, success is within your grasp. With a lot of effort on your part, an effective plan of action, and appropriate follow through, your success is assured.

Review this book and your completed exercises on a regular basis to keep the principles fresh in your mind. Continue doing those exercises that assist you in changing negative to positive.

Make use of this book as a workbook. Each time you chose a goal or success, go back through the book and apply the exercises in order to achieve the best success at the fastest rate.

Remember, your success begins in your mind. In truth, it is achieved in the mind, as well.

Change Your Mind — Change Your Life!

Lightning Source UK Ltd.
Milton Keynes UK
UKHW021015220221
379175UK00001B/58